Business Startup:

*Use Your Computer To Make $10,000
Per Month Through Multiple Passive
Income Business Opportunities*

Table of Contents

The follow Book is reproduced below with the goal of providing information that is as accurate and reliable as possible. Regardless, purchasing this Book can be seen as consent to the fact that both the publisher and the author of this book are in no way experts on the topics discussed within and that any recommendations or suggestions that are made herein are for entertainment purposes only. Professionals should be consulted as needed prior to undertaking any of the action endorsed herein.

This declaration is deemed fair and valid by both the American Bar Association and the Committee of Publishers Association and is legally binding throughout the United States.

Furthermore, the transmission, duplication or reproduction of any of the following work including specific information will be considered an illegal act irrespective of if it is done electronically or in print. This extends to creating a secondary or tertiary copy of the work or a recorded copy and is only allowed with express written consent from the Publisher. All additional right reserved.

The information in the following pages is broadly considered to be a truthful and accurate account of facts and as such any inattention, use or misuse of the information in question by the reader will render any resulting actions solely under their purview. There are no scenarios in which the publisher or the original author of this work can be in any fashion deemed liable for any hardship or damages that may befall them after undertaking information described herein.

Additionally, the information in the following pages is intended only for informational purposes and should thus be thought of as universal. As befitting its nature, it is presented without assurance regarding its prolonged validity or interim quality. Trademarks that are mentioned are done without written consent and can in no way be considered an endorsement from the trademark holder.

Introduction

Congratulations on acquiring **Business Startup** and thank you for doing so.

The following chapters will discuss how to make money via passive online business opportunities. These opportunities will come in multiple shapes and forms and hopefully I'll turn you on to things you'd never heard of before that will enable you to make quite a bit of extra money.

There are plenty of books on this subject on the market, thanks again for choosing this one! Every effort was made to ensure it is full of as much useful information as possible, please enjoy!

Chapter 1:
The Dream

It's the dream, right? Make tons of money without ever leaving your doorstep. It's like a early permanent retirement. In fact, it feels like a pipe dream.

But what if it isn't?

Before the internet, it was much harder. There were few work from home opportunities, of course, because telecom had hardly been developed at all yet.

But now that the internet is around, you have a constant connection to about three and a half billion people worldwide. These people have the ability to interconnect with one another over various niches, and they often will do exactly that.

These niches carry many faces and themes, but inevitably they will crop up. There are communities for everything these days, and likewise if there isn't a blog about something specific, then there will be.

In addition, there will always be people within these niches trying to take the new spot as "king of the internet" hill. They'll start producing content and constantly putting new things out there and eventually they'll take the place of the current head honcho, if they're good enough.

What results is that there are a ton of content creators competing in the tense stratosphere of the internet. Companies want to use that to their advantage and be on people's mouths as much as possible. If you've got the right online presence, you can use these companies in order to bring yourself a paycheck.

There are multiple ways about going into this that we're going to cover. This book is as much about building your online presence as it is about anything else. We're going to jump, first, into the world of affiliate marketing, specifically utilizing JvZoo and ClickBank. From there, we're going to jump over to e-mail marketing and building a mailing list to bring you profit and keep your users coming back. Then we're going into dropshipping and how you can utilize it in your advantage by creating a storefront online. Finally, we're going to jump into creating a blog in order to help you do all of the former, wrapping them up into one neat little package that people can go to online and find everything they need for your niche - in turn making a bunch of profit for you.

Before we go into the exact details, I'm going to take a second to go off on a tangent about how big of a deal motivation will be in this whole process. Motivation will make the difference between making zero dollars per month and making thousands. We're not talking in terms of cents. We're talking about real, hard cash that can be in your hands. Motivation is what's going to determine everything. I can teach you how to make all the content you want and how to utilise that content in order to bring in money, but it's up to you to actually make the content and do the things that are going to make you money. We said *passive* money, which it will certainly be after a while, but just like with any kind of passive money, it is going to take initial time on your part.

If you follow my advice closely then you can expect to bring in a ton of money after a while. These are not rocket science, nor are they witch brews. These are real proven methods for bringing in extra money, and the proof is in the pudding.

By the end of this book, I intend to help you be a very effective content creator who, if you utilize these opportunities correctly, can bring in a pretty big sum of money every month.

Chapter 2:
Affiliate Marketing

Affiliate marketing encompasses a very broad spectrum of activity but comes down to one simple activity: you getting rewarded for having viewers.

Affiliate marketing is essentially when a business rewards you for bringing them visitors by your own marketing methods. The way that they reward you can vary, but we'll jump into that momentarily.

This specific brand of marketing can take many forms. The gist is that there are people out there who want their products sold and advertised, and they're willing to pay well for people willing to take that job up for them.

There are tons of companies out there that are just looking for talented writers and content creators willing to write about their products and bring them new customers. In affiliate marketing, that'd be your job.

There are a few different modes of pay.

The most predominant mode is pay per sale, which means you get a portion of every sale they make. As your site generates more traffic, this can actually make a pretty huge difference. The sale commission programs tend to be anywhere between five percent and twenty percent, though some go even higher.

Another mode of payment is the *cost per action* mechanism, also known as *cost per acquisition* or *cost per conversion* . The way that this works is that you are paid for every specified acquisition. These can range in form from impression to form submissions or clicks.

Those are the two primary modes of payment. However, other forms of payment that are utilized are *cost per click* and *cost per mille*.

The way that *cost per click* works is that you will backlink and you'll actually get paid for every time that a link is clicked. These links can have various forms but this form is a bit antiquated and also not nearly as much of a money maker, and thus I don't recommend it. Cost per click payments can actually drive away whoever is reading your content, as it will make them feel they're being advertised to and make them less likely to return. The human psyche hates to feel like it's being manipulated, so avoid anything that will make them feel like they're just a tool for you to make money.

Cost per mille may be familiar as the payment form used by popular video sharing platform YouTube. This method will pay you according to how many views you attract, either on your site for a specific article or how many views they get to their site from a backlink via your site.

Affiliate marketing can be an extremely effective method of making money. I've heard a few anecdotal cases of people making upwards of thirty five thousand dollars *per month* from affiliate marketing. Of course, if you're just starting out, you can't expect to make nearly that much. Consider, though, that as you keep going with it, you'll build more and more traffic and have more and more people clicking the links you provide, making a ton of potential sales for you.

With the main methods of pay covered, I'm now going to cover the two affiliate marketing sites that I've found to be most effective: JvZoo and Clickbank.

JvZoo is an excellent starting point in your affiliate marketing adventure. Self-described as the "global technology that drives online sales", they aim to "help [the user] build a successful and profitable internet business."

It's free to become an affiliate at JvZoo and they'll provide you any and all training. Commissions are instantly paid. They're fantastic because they offer real-time tracking of your traffic and your earning statistics, as well as an instant sale notification. This can be a godsend and also a massive motivator as you're going forward. As we've already touched on, motivation can be a massive factor in determining exactly how much you make every month.

Working with JvZoo is simple. You just sign up, and then you have access to their entire affiliate product library. We'll talk more about finding a niche later, but finding a niche is going to be super simple with JvZoo.

The other primary option and route that you could go is ClickBank. ClickBank is a long-established affiliate marketing service. To quote their site, "for 17 years, [Clickbank has] partnered with digital marketers like you to sell [their] products to over 200 million customers around the globe".

ClickBank offers commissions as high as 75%. They don't offer immediate payment, like JvZoo does, but you *can* choose to get paid as often as every week. They also have a tracking system which ensures that you get paid even if a customer waits to purchase after clicking the link that you provide.

Another fantastic thing about ClickBank is that a great many of the products and services they offer are sold on a recurring subscription basis. This is a fantastic opportunity for you, because they will allow you to constantly get a commission, month after month or year after year.

ClickBank also offers a system by which you can set up joint ventures, allowing you to split the profits that you make with other partners. You can set up contracts for payment sharing, and ClickBank will handle the rest, making collaboration easy-peasy if you decide that you want to go into an affiliate marketing venture with somebody else.

In addition to that, ClickBank also has a very advanced analytic system which will give you access to details about impressions and clicks, as well as fine details about every last sale that you make. This will help you to create a better marketing campaign or market your products in your content better.

The beauty of affiliate marketing is that a lot of is left to you. You're essentially given a blank canvas, allowed to paint how you please. All that matters at the end of the day is that you draw sales to your clients somehow. It just so happens that affiliate marketing goes hand in hand with content creation. We'll tap more into this angelic combination in the last chapter of the book concerning how to tie all of the concepts we've delved into together with a blog or website that you set up yourself.

Before we move onto the next part of the book, I'd like to show you just how tasteful and well-done affiliate marketing can be.

MoneySavingExpert.com. Heard of it? If not, then you've been missing out. This site fills a very specific niche. It started in 2003 and was one of the first major sites to blow up while utilizing affiliate marketing. It has a simple goal: helping people handle their money better.

A modest site, a modest start. It's a huge force now Their facebook has seventy-seven *thousand* likes. Their twitter has *two hundred and twenty-eight thousand* followers. That's a big deal, friend. A very, very big deal. People have linked back to them 918,000 times. Their Alexa rank - their overall ranking on the Web in terms of traffic - is 1,901. They have a mailing list of 10,000,000 people.

They've generated a lot of traffic and, naturally, a lot of revenue. They employ 80 people, which is a lot of money in salaries. A lot.

But believe it or not, they don't run any ads, nor do they ever charge somebody for using the site. The sole way that they make their money is through the use of affiliate programs, and they're also very transparent about their use of such links.

Chapter 3:
Email Marketing

This one seems obvious, but it's hugely profitable to those who do it correctly.

You might hear email marketing and think "spam" but this isn't always the case. Email marketing can be massively beneficial to both the end-user and the sender. Consider Bernie Sanders' presidential campaign. He would often send out campaign emails with a big donate button, and talk about current affairs. Through this, he generated millions of dollars and inspired millions of people, many of whom would become activists for certain causes that they consider important.

Whether you agree with his politics or not, that's an example of email marketing done right. It didn't make the user feel like they were being spammed. It made them feel like they were part of an inclusive group of people that were making a change.

Email marketing can be used in several different ways. They can be used to directly promote a product, or you can use them to encourage customer loyalty and return visits to your site by way of a mailing list.

Mailing lists are incredibly important in today's online world. It's estimated that there are about two and a half billion email users worldwide. Of course not all of those are going to speak English and gravitate towards whatever niche you provide, but still. The point is there and very apparent: email marketing is going to be a massive force for you in your profit generation.

One of your big goals should be building your mailing list. A list is crucial to having return visitors and ensuring that people return to your site. Creating a site with great content is half the battle. Making people want to come back and read more is the other half.

When you create a mailing list you enable yourself to reach your readers again and again.

If you do it right, a mailing list and, by extension, email marketing can be incredibly effective. There are some big no-nos with email lists, though.

The biggest is constantly sending emails. This is how you find your way into a spam filter. I'm saying this not to bring politics into this book, but to give an example: I'm a supporter of the Green Party. I follow them actively and try to be involved with them. However, I'm unsubscribed from their mailing list. They send emails constantly, and the emails tend to be along the same lines all of the time. An occasional e-mail or even a regular e-mail once per week will be incredibly effective without driving anybody off.

The other primary thing to avoid is doing things in your emails which will lead to people unsubscribing. I don't know about you, but I personally don't want my inbox cluttered with emails that just beg me to buy this thing or that in order to make a profit off of me. I don't want to be begged or coerced into buying something every time I open my inbox, and if a company were to send me e-mails like that all the time, I'd unsubscribe from their mailing list.

Think of it like you were the end user. If you joined a mailing list, why would you? You would join it because you like the products or services that they offer, correct? Or possibly the content that they create, correct? Correct. In short, you'd join because you wanted to hear more from them in the future, and see what other things they'll have.

Then think about what kind of email you'd like to receive.

Here's how I would (and do) structure my emails. Note this is just a personal guideline that I follow, and isn't necessarily what you should do. Use your own judgment:

- **TITLE**: Avoid using something obnoxious. Start out with your name in all-caps or some other eye-catching way so they know who it's from, then a colon, then a short summary of your email or a catchy title. If you owned a content geared towards food, you could have your title be something like "THE SALTED SOUP: New recipes, week of 10/28/16" or "THE SALTED SOUP: Hot dog, hot diggity dog!". It doesn't have to be obnoxious and all-capital and scream "HEY LOOK AT ME". People are well aware that people who send them emails want them to be read, and people are pretty simple too: if you're begging them to do something, they often won't. All you have to do is present that you're sending them something. They'll do the rest.

- **OPENER:** Act familiar, like the people you're sending the email to are your family. Say "Hey, [name], this is a little update from The Salted Soup, giving you the scoop on what's new this week/month".

- **AFFILIATE PRODUCT OFFERS:** If you're going to include an affiliate product offer (you crass, sly dog, you), make it subtle and understated. Throw it in your closer, almost like an afterthought. This makes it seem like you aren't just writing them to have them make money for you. After all, you're not. You're writing to maintain some kind of connection with your userbase. Say something along the lines of "Well, that's it for this week. Before I go, I wanna recommend that you check out [product]. It's [short sentence, few nice sounding adjectives, say good things about the product].

- **STORE UPDATES/SALES:** You can tactfully include store updates if you primarily run a store and they subscribe to your mailing list, or include price cuts if you're running a sale. I'd recommend no more than three products in any given e-mail, and don't drone on about them or copy their entire description. Rather, write something simple about each product, why they were worth adding to your store, things of that nature.

- **CONTENT OF THE EMAIL:** Keep it conversational. These people aren't robots. A lot of the time, they're native English speakers just like you. There's a reason it's in vogue in "Silicon Valley"-style copywriting to make it sound very casual and conversational. It sounds incredibly non-threatening and builds an automatic rapport with youthful users. If you're older, don't intentionally try to sound youthful. Just talk how you talk. Don't speak pretentiously, don't use a thesaurus, just say what you yourself would say.

- **CONTENT UPDATES:** If you run a blog, advertising new content in your emails can be an effective way to draw views from your mailing list. There are two ways I like to do this. The first is to mention them casually: "We also added x this week, an article about y, and I think you'll like it a lot," would be a great and simple line that will still catch attention. Another way is to make a bulleted list of new updates with short summaries. If you run a blog and they're subscribed, you've probably already got it relatively in the bag as far as getting them to view your new content.

Historically, the most effective email marketing techniques come in two camps: the provocative, and the non-provocative. You can decide for yourself which to go for. Either way, the goal in email marketing is to not be one of those content creators that sends constant material to their subscribers and makes them not want to subscribe anymore. This is such a valuable tool that will put dedicated users right under your fingers every time you send out a mass mail.

The example above, for the record, is just my own and the way that I would do things. For a second, I want to look at other massively successful email marketing campaigns.

Something that can be very effective in email marketing is to be creative. If you're a naturally creative person, use it to your advantage. For example, charity: water has done this. When you donate to them, you can actually get a timeline of your money and where exactly it's going. This makes you feel more connected to the entire process and also feel like you're making a difference. It's a gorgeously executed piece of marketing that will make you want to donate even more.

I said earlier that simply sending out promotional emails isn't the best idea, but if executed correctly, it can be really really effective, too. Consider Uber. They don't really waste time. They show a promotion at the top, and below that, they explain it. The former part is perfect for people who simply would like to skim their emails and determine if it's worth reading or not, and the latter part is great for informing them if they are interested. It's simple and very effective.

One thing to take away from the Uber email marketing campaign is that simplicity speaks. Another great example of this is *Poncho*. *Poncho* is a daily subscription service which sends you the weather. However, it doesn't overdo it on the details. It offers quick and important information in a funny and cute way that makes it a pleasure to read every single day.

The key to a strong email is your copy. This is the reason for my obsession with being personable and approachable in my emails, and the reason that other email marketing schemes - simple and complex - succeed. Good copy is essential to all marketing and can make the difference between your emails being instantly archived or a joy to read every single time.

The internet is big and growing every single day. Now is a better time than ever to take advantage of email marketing. It's practically a necessity in the modern world to have an email, and as Earth develops, eventually virtually everybody will have access to email. Even right now, there's a massive number of people with email. Not taking advantage of this opportunity to grow your brand is absolutely criminal and entirely shortsighted. You owe it to yourself and your venture to learn how to write proper email copy and take advantage of the enormous potential of email marketing and mailing lists.

Chapter 4:
Dropshipping

Tangentially related to all of this, yet equally as valuable, is the idea of dropshipping. Dropshipping is essentially where a retailer doesn't keep items in stock themselves but forwards orders and shipping details for the purchase to another entity. This entity could be either another retailer, a manufacturer, or a wholesaler.

There are two primary ways to make a profit via dropshipping: the first is that the retailer, like in an actual store, simply sells the item for higher than the wholesale price. The other way is that you make a sale commission, paid to you by the wholesaler.

The latter is the way that we're going to focus on here, utilizing a service called Shopify.

Shopify is a major e-commerce company, relatively young as far as tech companies go, founded only in 2004.

The reason Shopify is important is because they make it super simple to open an online store. You're going to take advantage of this opportunity in order to make money.

The next thing to do is to find a wholesaler, selling a product that you'd like to sell, and then get in contact with them about dropshipping. You can do this with numerous different products and figure out how they deal with dropshipping. Shopify has a fantastic FAQ on this which lists attributes of great wholesale supplies:

- **Expert staff**

  - Good dropshippers will have knowledgeable sales reps who know the products that they create and are invaluable when you need assistance.

- **Dedicated support**

  - Good dropshippers will have fantastic support staff, often an individual assigned to you, that will take care of you and any problems you may face.

- **Technologically invested**

  - Good dropshippers will generally be strongly invested in tech and will have things like real-time inventory and an exhaustive catalog that will make your job far easier.

- **Accept email orders**

  - Good dropshippers won't require you to call in every order or place it on their site, which will save a lot of time.

- **Central location**

  - Good dropshippers will be in the middle of the country so that your packages can reach their destinations quickly no matter where they're heading.

- **Organized**

  - Good dropshippers will have efficient systems and intelligent staff who know what they're talking about. Not-so-good dropshippers will mess up orders and infuriate you.

You want to search for a dropshipper with these attributes, as it will make your job a lot easier. One that I personally recommend you use is AliExpress. The reason that I recommend them is because they are absolutely huge, and have a ton of products that you sell on your store. It's incredibly easy to set up dropshipping with AliExpress because people on there simply want to sell their products and AliExpress realizes that this is a factor.

So for the sake of simplicity, I'm going to use AliExpress as an example.

The next thing that you do is set up your online store using Shopify and add whatever products on AliExpress you want to be on your store.

It's worthwhile to take a bit of extra time considering what products you want to sell. Some products are far better than others. For example, avoid selling knockoffs, and sell things that you can find a high profit margin on. If your niche were phone accessories, for example, you could find a phone case on AliExpress for incredibly cheap - say, a silicon case for $3. You could sell this on your store for $7. You then make a 133% profit margin, and this is going to make a huge deal.

It's imperative when you're setting up your online store that you write your own descriptions and make everything unique. See, when you set up an online store, the thing that's going to set you apart isn't whether you can offer a product at the most competitive price or not. If people want the cheapest price, they can just go to a wholesaler. What will set you apart is your ability to broadcast yourself and put yourself out there, as well as your ability to create a trustworthy retail image.

Note that you don't have to price gouge everything. You can absolutely sell the product at about 150% and still make a fair amount of money, especially if you get a lot of traffic. There are other factors, too, of course, but this can make a huge difference between you and the next seller. A difference of five dollars may not seem like much, but it can make the difference between having a sale or not having a sale in a huge number of cases.

Dropshipping is actually a really beautiful system and a super easy way to make money because you don't actually have to keep any inventory yourself. All you're doing is acting as a middleman between the wholesaler and the buyer. There's nothing wrong with this. Places like Walmart do the same thing in the real world.

Chapter 5:
Implementing all the Methods

This chapter is intended to tie in a lot of what we've talked about up to here in the context of a blog. For the purpose of example, we're going to be utilizing Wordpress because Wordpress is widely used and widely supported. However, you could use any blog platform you'd like to. The end goal isn't getting a site established; it's creating effective content that people are going to not only want to read but want to share and want to come back to when you create more content. Getting a site established is only a thoroughfare to that goal.

So the first thing you want to do when establishing a site is figure out your niche. There are a few different ways to do this, but the best way is to go to an affiliate marketing site and figure out what products you care about and can write about. Beware of saturated markets where your "niche" isn't really a "niche". Technology is a fantastic example. It would be super duper extremely hard to break into the realm of technology because there are already so many sites, big and small, geared for that exact niche.

The single best way to create a website which will spawn effective content that will help your affiliate marketing would be to do it on something you're passionate about to some degree. I can't repeat this enough. Your site will only do as well as your content. If you make clickbait content that hardly has any weight, people aren't going to click on your links or buy things that you ask them to.

Once you have your niche figured out, you really have two options from here.

You can find affiliate products that satisfy your niche and write your own articles about them, or you can find those affiliate products and outsource them to people that know your niche well.

There are advantages to both.

The advantages to the first are obvious: control. You know exactly the quality of the article you're putting out, you have a lot more control over everything that is said and written, and ultimately you get the final word (literally.)

The advantages to the other are that, if you don't know your niche as well as you'd like, or it's a very research-intensive niche such as vacuum cleaners, you can write broader articles and just outsource the major articles to other people.

As a writer myself, I personally prefer the first for obvious reasons. I love having creative control over everything that I put out, and I love deserving every last bit of what I've earned. Also, I don't have to pay other people in order to do my work, which means I get every penny from my site.

However, if you're not a writer or don't have a knack for making online sales pitches for the products that you're marketing, you very well may want to just outsource your articles. It's realistic that if your site picks up traction, the money you make from sales of the product will easily be a massive return investment.

There are people out there that understand any niche you can name. There have to be. That's why it's a niche, and that's why these products exist in the first place: people out there understand how to make them and how they work. So if you are in a research intensive niche or just making a site for a niche you don't understand very well, don't ever fear that you won't be able to attain quality content. You just may not be the one producing said content.

You do get some choice in the quality of your content, though. You can easily get one-off articles for very cheap on the internet. Professionally written articles and reviews will be about more expensive. It's not uncommon to see rates of $100 for a thousand words for quality writing. One fantastic resource for outsourcing your content, should you choose to go this route, is WriterAccess.com. They have a talented team of writers that cover a great variety of interests. They've got a six-star rating system that can at six-stars range from $0.10 to $2 per word. 5-star writers make eight cents per word, and every star-level below that makes two cents less per word, all the way two cents per word for 2-star writers. You certainly get what you pay for, and I can't recommend this site enough should you choose to go that route.

The content is the key to any and all affiliate marketing. Content is going to decide whether a person buys the affiliate product or not. Just as important as content, however, is timing.

Pay special attention to holidays such as Christmas and Hannukah. The most sales will happen, of course, when it's a time for giving. Launching a review or blog post about a major product release or "twenty great cheap holiday gifts" will bring the orders a-flowin' and you'll be making tons of cash off of it. If your site has a food niche, then you could very easily write holiday recipes and offer affiliate links to ingredients. The stopgap with this is that, of course, you'll have to have tried them yourself. However, if you have a delicious recipe that gets used and people buy the product you promote, the investment will easily pay off in no time. If you get a twenty-five percent sales commission then all it takes is four sales of an item in order to make that money book. Anything on top of that is pure profit.

After you've figured out your niche and wrapped your head around affiliate marketing, you can start to focus on your Shopify store. You need to set one up, of course, and give it the same name as your blog.

The great thing about Shopify is that you can actually use it on your own domain and link to it from your site, which will make it super simple for people to find.

With the niche that you set up earlier, you can set up your own store that caters to said niche. For example, if you have a coffee niche, you can set up your own store that dropships products such as mugs or coffee scoops and bag clips. You could also sell exotic coffee beans or coffee grinders. Really, you just need to identify products on AliExpress that you can incorporate into your content and sell these on your online store at a rate which will draw you a profit.

Going further on the coffee niche, if your blog had a recipe for, say, a raspberry vanilla frozen latte, you could have an equipment list at the beginning of the post, as such:

THE NeatBeans RASPBERRY VANILLA FROZEN LATTE

by John Doe

EQUIPMENT:

- Milk frother

- Espresso machine

- Blender

If the espresso machine and the blender affiliate offers, you could promote them by linking them directly. After the equipment list, you could say "if you don't have a milk frother, you can buy them from the NeatBeans store where we sell professional coffee supplies for cheap prices!" Users could then follow the link and place an order from the milk frother.

The beauty of the affiliate sales and the Shopify store is that they synergize so perfectly. They make your blog more than a place to go for recipes or advice or reviews. Suddenly, it becomes a one-stop shop for anything that they need related to the topic that you (or somebody you hire) are producing content about.

Giving your readers access to anything that they may need, as well as ensuring that your content is as quality as it can possibly be, will be a huge factor in assuring that you not only gain readers but retain them as well.

Another way by which you can retain your writers is by setting up a mailing list. As I wrote earlier, this is incredibly essential and there really is no way to understate the importance of maintaining a mailing list.

There are three primary ways to grow a mailing list. The first is to simply offer your users the chance to join a mailing list somewhere on your page. This is generally the most effective. You can offer free content in return, or simply ask them to join in the first place. If they like your content, they will join. Give them the opportunity in the middle of every article with a line or box that reads something like "Like what you're reading? Join our mailing list to get updates!". As we said earlier, spam is a huge no-no, so you can honestly tell them that you hate spam as much as they do, and they can expect to not be spammed if they sign up. Nobody likes spam.

Related to the first but a tad more intricate is to have a pop-up when a user opens an article or scrolls past a certain point. It should be similar. Since it's a pop-up, you have a fair bit more freedom design wise with it. It doesn't have to be anything spectacular. It can just be a simple box with two text fields in which the user types their name and email address and that's that. This has a lot of flair and makes you look more professional if done right. It's also a very "Web 2.0" thing to do and is prevalent in modern web design for new companies.

The other way to grow a mailing list is to mailgate your content. This is relatively simple. The first step is to have strong and addictive content on your site that is free to read and explore. Link, however, to your site from within itself (this helps with search engine optimization, too) to articles that are behind what I suppose you could call a "free paywall": allow the reader to access your site and all of its content, but ask that they provide their email and join your mailing list first.

It doesn't quite matter how you set your mailing list up. All that matters is that you do. Once you do, it's time to start working on writing effective copy that will grab people's attention.

As I said earlier, your copy is everything - especially in your emails. This is much like your blog in that there is *no* shame in outsourcing it if you're unable to write solid copy. I was once a freelance writer myself, and I can say for certain that I would have without a doubt taken a gig where I wrote weekly copy for email for a decent rate. For a short email, the rate doesn't even have to be terribly high. This is another thing where the investment will pay off, especially if you find a writer that's willing to do it cheaply.

Your blog will be the pinnacle of, as well as the focal point to, your online presence. It should be where everything you do meets like lines from an origin point.Your social media sites should all link back to it. There's the extra advantage that linking to your site from social media counts as a backlink which will make it more popular on search engines. This will be massively beneficial to your online presence in the long run, but we'll cover that more in the next chapter.

Your store will be connected to, and optimally hosted on the same domain as, your blog. This, combined with your affiliate links, will form the bulk of the income you'll be making doing this method, so it's super important that you do everything you can to make your store presentable and keep it maintained. Theoretically you don't have to do the store option, but that's for you to decide. It's nice for the reason I provided earlier: you can provide a one stop shop for your niche, in a sense.

When you make a blog about a niche, you're no longer just throwing around a business idea. You're becoming a spokesperson for that niche, and somewhat of an authority for people that are newcomers to it. There's a certain amount of reverence and respectability to that, and you should know that and feel great about it.

As you post more and more on your blog, the more passive income you'll gain. Blog posts don't stick around from week to week. They, and the affiliate links contained therein, stick around constantly. Logically, the more blog posts that you have and the more affiliate products or dropshipped items you have available, the more money you'll be making.

The point of saying that is to say that starting up this blog isn't going to be the easiest thing ever at first. Like anything worth doing, it will take time and effort and a fair amount of personal exertion. There's where the passion for your niche comes in and will help you propel yourself through the initial pain and tediousness of starting up a blog with affiliate programs and content worth reading.

But I can say from my personal experience using these methods in order to make money that it will be worth it.

Chapter 6:
Ensuring Your Success

There is no easy road to success. Anybody who says this is a liar, through and through. Some successes come easier than others, though, and some success comes by absolute luck. You shouldn't rely on luck for your success though. Most success comes through one thing alone: work.

There are a few tricks you can use to help ensure your blog's success.

The first major thing I would do in your shoes is, if you don't already know much about it, learn about search engine optimization.

Search engine optimization is what will take your site to the top of Google search when people look up certain keywords.

There are people out there that will try to tell you a million and a half things about search engine optimization that won't really help. There are even people out there that will try to sell you links in order to "increase your search engine ranking". Be wary. The way that search engines work is actually really simple.

Search engines scour the web for certain things every time a search query is made. When your page is out there, published and on the web, it will come up in certain search results on any search engine. The goal of search engine optimization is to bring your page specifically up in the rankings so that it will be viewed more often by people looking into the topic.

These search engine spiders will rank your site compared to others based off of a few key concepts. The key thing that they're always looking for is the relevancy your site serves to the search query, so it wants to return the most relevant site. The first part of relevancy is, of course, content. Keywords are important, but overusing them is a bad idea and will only serve to make your content less readable. Titles and metadata descriptions are as important, if not more.

It also ranks higher pages that are quick and work well, obviously. If I were the developer of a search engine, the last thing I'd want it to do is route people to websites that are dysfunctional, shabbily put together, and altogether incondite.

Then it scans to see how much of an authority your site is. Being linked to from other sites, or having information that is good enough to be linked to, is important. The more your site is referenced elsewhere, the higher that it's going to be ranked in authority.

The last and final thing by which they determine relevancy is your user experience. Your site being easy to navigate and get around is essential. Not only will it attract more users in the first place by being easy to understand and navigate, it will actually lead to people being on your site for longer. This will also help to reduce your bounce rate. Bounce rate is defined as "the percentage of visitors to a particular website who navigate away from the site after viewing only one page". This is a critical issue, and you need to do everything you can to minimize it, but we'll get to that in a second. Having the best and most intuitive user interface you possibly can will go a long way towards reducing your bounce rate.

Search engine optimization is very key to having a successful website and can make a gargantuan difference in the level of traffic that you can see. There are individuals who are dedicated to optimizing your sites for search, but if you'd like to do it yourself, there are actually lots of online courses for it. There's only so much I can reasonably cover in this book because, well, it's not a search engine optimization book, it's a book about creating a website and making money passively. But there is a ton of free information available on the internet for search engine optimization. Examples include SEO by the Sea and WebmasterWorld.

Beyond search engine optimization, there are a few other ways to increase your traffic.

The most obvious is advertising. It seems to go without saying but it can really make a huge difference, and is more approachable than it used to be, too. The days of sketchy Google AdSense being your best friend are over. There are a lot of new technologies you can use to your advantage.

One of these is social media. Social media is now your new best friend (bye-bye, AdSense!) in two different ways.

The first is in an advertising sense. The ability to promote your tweets and Facebook posts is going to be massively useful going forward, and are one of the biggest advancements for small businesses that these social media platforms have put forward. They also have standard old-school advertising, where their models may differ a bit. Generally, due to the sheer size of major social media platforms, their advertising rates are exorbitant. If you can afford them, though, they can be a massive boost to your business.

The second is in a general outreach sense, which will keep you connected to your customers and readers and keep you in their minds. This is essential to having return site visitors and can also gain you a lot of traction when your current followers share your posts with new potential ones.

The very nature of social media also opens it up to a very organic method of free advertisement. We live in an age of share, share, share which works out perfectly for you because that's *exactly* what you want. Social media is built upon sharing with one another and all it takes is the right post gaining traction or going viral to gain visitors in the thousands or even millions.

To this end, some social media platforms are better than others. On Facebook, for example, only two percent of your fans generally will see any given post that you make on the platform. Instagram, on the other hand, puts it in the feed of everybody that follows you. This means that for certain niches - especially those that are popular among youth and naturally more photogenic such as botanical niches - will be very well suited by Instagram and, in turn, treated well by using said platform. Snapchat, similarly, will share snaps on your story with all of your friends and is very well suited to things that are more photogenic in nature.

Regardless of the potential advertising benefits of social media though, you need to make a page for your business on at least Facebook, Twitter, and Instagram. This is partly because they provide another means for your users to contact you beyond e-mail. But it's mainly because social media is the ultimate platform for any business. It allows you to congregate everybody who loves your service and content into a few central hubs to be reached in one capacity or another. Also, if you have 10,000 facebook fans, only 2,000 may see a post you make - *but*, you can use a feature known as post promotion which is very cheap but can widen the audience that you reach by massive, massive amounts.

The single biggest thing in ensuring your success though is to do everything you can to generate quality content.

I've parroted all of this before, but it's endlessly true. The biggest thing you can do for yourself in the world of online content creation is make sure your content sticks out and makes a name for itself. Whether this means buckling down and making something great or outsourcing it to people who are willing to do that, it needs to be done. The quality of the content can and will make a double-digit difference in the amount of people who buy any affiliate product you suggest. Quality content will also make people more likely to trust your blog enough to buy from your Shopify store. Who wants to buy from somebody who can't even publish a half-decent article about what they're trying to sell?

On a related note, headlines are insanely important. If the content of the article is important to making sales and keeping readers, the headline is important to getting those readers in the first place. The headline is what intrigues a person enough to read something. Your titles don't have to be clickbait at all, but they do have to be intriguing and hook people.

Having super strong headlines will also play a role in your bounce rate, which will in turn conversely affect your search engine ranking. Funny how that works, right? Imagine this: someone falls on your site's landing page somehow. Are they likely to keep going if every headline bores them to death? No. They'll leave and your bounce rate will go up.

Places that are centered around making shareable viral content such as Buzzfeed and Upworthy will write down double-digit headlines before finally deciding on one that will drive the most traffic. Headlines are terribly important in any sort of content creation, and skimping over them is a fatal error. They can and will make or break how attractive your site is for any new visitor. They can and will decide whether people will click on the Facebook post you promoted. It doesn't matter how many people follow you if they don't click on the things that you put out there.

The last big thing, and I've said it before, is to apply your passions to this entire project.

There's a saying about novelists: "the successful ones write what they know."

Have you ever read a book and it was written by someone who had a good idea but felt totally out of their element because they had no idea *really* what it was like to be in the position of any of their characters and so the story felt very contrived and the book was hardly worth the paper it was printed on? That comes across everywhere.

If you try to make a site based around a niche that you just altogether don't care about, it's going to come across that you don't care about it. Not because your writing is necessarily bad, but simply because when somebody cares about something, it's *very* apparent. They'll write with energy and gusto and won't be able to wait between one line and the next, they'll blaze through everything and you'll be able to somehow read in their writing that they're impassioned about it. The most successful blogs are written by people that are passionate about what they're writing about.

Take for example blogs about the ketogenic diet. The ketogenic diet is very niche, yes, and genuinely delicious recipes are hard to come by since the diet and related content only appeals to people that are doing low-carb diets, but sites like I Breathe, I'm Hungry don't skip a beat when it comes to constantly putting out quality keto-friendly content. In theory, they probably could have monetized more by doing something more popular if they caught the same kind of traction. However, the fact that they're passionate about what they do comes across in the fact that despite their topic being incredibly niche, they are putting out quality content ALL of the time and hardly ever falter in their ability to provide great and delicious recipes for individuals following keto, paleo, or other related diets, as well as for people on gluten-free diets. The thing that will most guide the quality of the content that you personally put forth is always going to be passion, before knowledge or before anything else. Passion will guide you to knowledge, because you care enough to learn. Passion will guide you to inspiration, because you burn for something and find it in a lot of what you do.

Referring back to I Breathe, I'm Hungry, t's also important to note that part of the fact that they're doing so well is *because* of the fact that they're so niche, yet so impassioned. That's the biggest thing you can do. Find something you care about that the niche hasn't been filled for yet.

But that's just a way for you to ensure that you will grow. If you want to take your chances by just finding a niche and starting, then you absolutely can, and you absolutely could find success. But writing on your passions will naturally increase your chances of creating something worth reading for obvious reasons.

The biggest thing that will increase traffic to your site is your personal devotion to the content thereof.

Now we're nearing the end of the book and I feel like there are some things that I have to drive home before we conclude. First off, thanks for sticking with me throughout this, it's a lot to read and soak in about something that's really pretty simple.

I think with all of my heart that these methods work. You're not glued to any part of it, though. I'm not here to hold your hand and make you do anything. I'm here to give you the guideline by which I did something cool. That doesn't mean you can't do something cool completely of your own accord, and if I enable you or inspire you to do something great and something worthwhile then that's fantastic and I'm super proud and happy.

Ultimately, friend, this is your adventure. I can give you all the links and things to Google that I want, but doing so won't automatically give you results. Anything you do will involve a fair amount of trial and error and finding your own way.

You don't have to fill out emails the way I did or use the same exact affiliate programs, and you don't have to use a WordPress blog or stick to any one very specific and boxed-in niche, really.

The decisions that you will make are yours, and it's up to you to make the right decisions for the situation that you're in. I just hope I've helped to shed some light and that in a year, you'll be glad that you read this book and followed any instructions that you may have chosen to.

Conclusion

Thank for making it through to the end of *Business Startup*, let's hope it was informative and able to provide you with all of the tools you need to achieve your goals.

The next step is to apply this knowledge. This book isn't much of a reference, but you can certainly use it as one and refer back to it as you need. I'm not guru and I'm not some kind of Messianic figure or online start-up company evangelist. I'm just someone who uses these methods to success, and has seen other people use the same ones to success. I genuinely think that the system I've developed and the way that these things interconnect is fantastic and will work for you as well, reader. So with that said, the next thing that you need to do is go out and start applying this. Browse affiliate product offers on JvZoo or ClickBank or wherever in order to figure out your niche, then grab a WordPress blog and get to work. Things will only happen for you if you make them happen.

Finally, if you found this book useful in anyway, a review on Amazon is always appreciated! Thank you.

www.ingramcontent.com/pod-product-compliance
Lightning Source LLC
Chambersburg PA
CBHW061232180526
45170CB00003B/1264